W9-AUB-476

First Facts®

Inspired by Nature

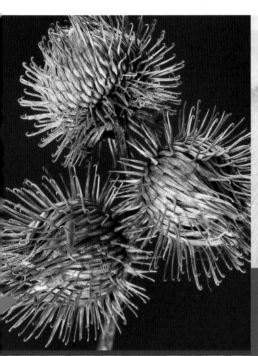

CLOTHING

Inspired by Nature

by Margeaux Weston

PEBBLE
a capstone imprint

First Facts is published by Pebble,
1710 Roe Crest Drive, North Mankato, Minnesota 56003
www.capstonepub.com

Library of Congress Cataloging-in-Publication Data
Names: Weston, Margeaux, author.
Title: Clothing inspired by nature / by Margeaux Weston.
Description: North Mankato, Minnesota : Pebble, [2020] | Series: Inspired by nature | Audience: Ages 6-9. | Audience: K to grade 3. | Includes bibliographical references and index.
Identifiers: LCCN 2019006444 | ISBN 9781977108371 (library binding) | ISBN 9781977110077 (pbk.) | ISBN 9781977108562 (ebook pdf)
Subjects: LCSH: Clothing and dress—Technological innovations—Juvenile literature. | Biomimicry—Juvenile literature. | Protective clothing—Juvenile literature. | Discoveries in science—Juvenile literature.
Classification: LCC TX355 .J6427 2020 | DDC 338.4/7687—dc23
LC record available at https://lccn.loc.gov/2019006444

Editorial Credits
Abby Colich and Jaclyn Jaycox, editors; Juliette Peters, designer;
Jo Miller, media researcher; Katy LaVigne, production specialist

Photo Credits
b=bottom, l=left, m=middle, r=right, t=top
iStockphoto: triloks, Cover; Newscom: Cal Sport Media/Bob Stanton, 9t, Kyodo/*, 15b, Supplied by WENN.com/ZOB/CB2, 19b; Science Source: Andrew J. Martinez, 17b, TService/Arno Vlooswijk, 11t; Shutterstock: chaphot, 13t, CharlotteRaboff, 21b, colin robert varndell, 1l, 7t, Dobo Kristian, 5, Ghan Saridnirun, 1r, 15t, Grigorev Mikhail, 17t, Jukka Jantunen, 21t, nico99, 19t, Praew stock, 13b, rbrown10, 1m, 11b, Stocksnapper, 7b, wildestanimal, 9b

Design Elements
Shutterstock: Zubada

Printed and bound in China.
001671

Table of Contents

From Nature to Clothes......................4

Hook and Loop Fastener....................6

Swim Like a Shark 8

Polar Bear Wear 10

Waterproof Leaves 12

Super Spinning Spiders....................14

Color Changing Creatures 16

Gecko Feet 18

Beaver Suits.................................20

Glossary 22

Read More 23

Internet Sites 23

Critical Thinking Questions 24

Index 24

From Nature to Clothes

Have you ever worn Velcro shoes? Would you like to wear clothes that change color? These ideas both came from nature. When ideas are copied from nature, it is called biomimicry. Nature **inspires** many things that improve our lives.

chemical—a substance used in or made by chemistry

inspire—to influence or encourage someone to do something

Fact
Scientists have found a use for a **chemical** in shrimp and crab shells. It stops sweaty clothes from smelling badly.

Hook and Loop Fastener

Have you ever had something stuck to your clothes? One inventor came home with **cockleburs** stuck to his pants. He studied the plants. They had small hooks. The hooks were stuck to the loops in the fabric. He created the hook and loop fastener in 1955. The fastener keeps shoes and other items closed. Velcro became a popular **brand** of hook and loop fastener.

---

brand—the company or name of a product

cocklebur—a plant that sheds prickly little balls

Swim Like a Shark

The great white shark is one of the fastest fish in the world. Shark skin has scales called **denticles**. They help sharks swim fast. Scientists studied the denticles. They made new swimsuits that are like a shark's skin. Scientists believe the suits make swimmers faster.

denticle—a small, toothlike scale that covers a shark's skin

Polar Bear Wear

Polar bears live in one of the coldest places in the world. Yet they stay warm. Tiny hairs trap heat. The hairs are **hollow** and filled with air. Scientists in China have designed a coat to work the same way. These coats will keep troops and firefighters warm.

hollow—empty on the inside

infrared—an invisible form of energy, such as heat

Invisible Bears

Infrared devices can see body heat in the dark. But polar bears are invisible to them. The temperature of a polar bear's outer coat matches the temperature of the air around it. Scientists are making clothing to work like these outer hairs. They may help people in militaries look invisible to enemies.

infrared image
of a polar bear

11

Waterproof Leaves

The leaves of a lotus plant are waterproof. A drop of water will roll off. The plant's leaves have tiny holes. They don't let the leaf absorb water. Scientists made a coating that works the same way. They put it on fabrics. It keeps fabric from getting soaked.

Fact

The lotus isn't just waterproof. It's dirtproof too! Scientists have made a paint that acts like the lotus petals. It keeps dirt away from walls.

Super Spinning Spiders

Golden silk orb weavers build the world's largest webs. The silk is very strong. It is also lightweight. Scientists made a material like the spider silk. It is used in shoes. The light material helps the shoes stay comfortable. Its strength helps them last longer.

Color Changing Creatures

Many animals can change color. They blend in with what's around them to hide from enemies. Scientists have studied how some sea animals, such as squid and zebrafish, do this. They are making a fabric to work the same way. Military members and hunters may be able to use this material to hide.

Fact

Scientists are making robots that will blend in with their surroundings. The robots can be used to study animals. They will be able to hide to avoid animal attacks.

zebrafish

squid

Gecko Feet

Geckos can run up and down walls without falling. They can even stick to a surface upside down! They do this with the help of tiny hairs on their feet. Scientists have made patches that work like gecko feet. When worn on the hands and feet, people can climb up walls!

space junk—man-made materials that are no longer useful and are orbiting Earth

Fact
Scientists plan to put arms like gecko feet on space robots. The robots will grab **space junk**.

Beaver Suits

Beavers jump in and out of water a lot. Yet they stay warm and dry. Their thick fur traps warm pockets of air. Surfers often go in and out of water too. Scientists created a rubber material that works like a beaver's fur. It may be used for **wet suits** to keep surfers warm and dry in cold water.

---

wet suit—a close-fitting suit made of material that keeps divers warm in cold water

20

Glossary

brand (BRAND)—the company or name of a product

chemical (KE-muh-kuhl)—a substance used in or made by chemistry

cocklebur (KOK-kuhl-ber)—a plant that sheds prickly little balls

denticle (DEN-tik-uhl)—a small, toothlike scale that covers a shark's skin

hollow (HAH-loh)—empty on the inside

infrared (in-fruh-RED)—an invisible form of energy, such as heat

inspire (in-SPIRE)—to influence or encourage someone to do something

space junk (SPAYSS JUHNGK)—man-made materials that are no longer useful and are orbiting Earth

wet suit (WET SOOT)—a close-fitting suit made of material that keeps divers warm in cold water

Read More

Kelsey, Elin. *Wild Ideas*. Berkeley, CA: Owlkids Books, Inc., 2015.

Koontz, Robin. *Nature Inspired Contraptions*. Nature-Inspired Innovations. Vero Beach, FL: Rourke Educational Media, 2018.

Lanier, Wendy Hinote. *Clothing Inspired by Nature*. Technology Inspired by Nature. Mendota Heights, MN: Focus Readers, 2018.

Internet Sites

14 Smart Inventions Inspired by Nature: Biomimicry
https://www.bloomberg.com/news/photo-essays/2015-02-23/14-smart-inventions-inspired-by-nature-biomimicry

How Biomimicry is Inspiring Human Innovation
https://thekidshouldseethis.com/post/31460154153

How We Make Stuff
https://www.made2bmadeagain.org/creatures_cwdtd

Critical Thinking Questions

1. Scientists designed a swimsuit that is like a shark's skin. How does this help the swimmer?

2. Reread page 12. Can you name some examples of when it would be useful to have waterproof fabric?

3. Reread page 18. When do you think it would be helpful for people to be able to climb walls?

Index

beavers, 20

biomimicry, 4

coats, 10

cockleburs, 6

fabrics, 6, 12, 16

geckos, 18

lotus plants, 12

paint, 12

polar bears, 10

robots, 16, 18

sharks, 8

silk, 14

spiders, 14

swimsuits, 8

Velcro, 6

wet suits, 20